I0622684

INTEGRITY

Book 2
of the

Carbon Copy Series

C. S. Phoenix

Paperback ISBN 979-8-98-553061-2

Cover Design: Chandra Watson

Book Illustration and Design: Rachel Ross

Author Photo: Marysol Onate

Praise for *Honor*

"C.S. Phoenix offers readers an invitation to explore challenging emotions as she unfolds her own internal battles. This is a raw and unfiltered ride on the road to resilience! I was glad to be a passenger."

- **Naketta Lowery**
  Trauma and Resilience Expert
  Sustainable Life Solutions LLC

"… I felt seen, and less alone as I worked my way through this book, and at times I teared up while reading it. Furthermore, I know I'll re-read it many times in the years to come, I loved it so much. I cannot recommend this enough for anyone who is struggling to love themselves, or wants to better understand a loved one who is."

- **Liliyanna Shadowlyn, The Faerie Review**

"Wow, truly breathtaking and raw - a book that was written from the heart of the author. A look into her life and experiences and how they helped shape her into her present being. I couldn't put this book down…"

- **LS, Amazon**

Also by C. S. Phoenix

Carbon Copy Series

Book 1 – Honor

Book 3 – Candor

This series is dedicated
To the younger versions of myself.
Thank you for surviving
So that we could learn to heal.
Thank you for finding a way
Through all the darkness and pain,
Long enough for us to become
The light we always needed.

You can rest now.

Acknowledgements

First and foremost, to my mom. I'm an adult now, with kids of my own, and I know you did the best you could with what you had. I love you. Thank you for trusting me to share my story even though it could not be easy on you. I am glad I finally had the courage to introduce my full self to you and build our relationship better than it has ever been. You are a queen and a hero, and you will always be an inspiration to me. Also thank you for rolling with the punches with me and helping me make this dream possible.

Rachel Ross, for sticking by my side for 20 plus years and being willing to roll with me on this project. You are a visionary and have helped bring my words to life. But before that, you gave me strength and courage over and over to continue to live this life. I feel like I will never really understand why or how we get along, but I think we have one of those loves that just doesn't need to be explained.

DJ Vinatieri (The Deege), I would not be here today had you not believed in me. You saw my strength, resilience, and potential when I could only see the barriers in front of me. You gave me the courage to believe in myself and become who I was meant to be. Thank you for your friendship. Broseph, you saved my life more times than I can count, and I will be forever grateful.

Sam Mobley, for offering your critique and editing so that I don't sound like a complete nimrod. I am so glad to have met you on this journey through life. Maybe one day I'll actually meet you in person.

Brenda Fowely, for giving me recording time to make this project possible on all fronts.

Mik, thank you for surviving our childhood and welcoming the story of how it looked from my perspective as I told you in adulthood. I'm glad we have become friends and we can put those nightmarish days behind us.

Kason, thank you for existing, first off. I know you had no part in it, but without you I don't know that I would have ever been given a reason to stop running and face my demons. Also, you are a dope little brother, and I am proud of all that you have done and been through in your short time on Earth. I can't wait to see what you become!

Flood

Screaming
Wailing

The sounds of a child
Coming from my
Very adult mouth

I heard them and tried to laugh
But more
Ear splitting cries
Emptied themselves from my throat

They had been hidden there for so long
Once the gates to my personal hell
Opened
They couldn't help but flood out

 # Bastard

I may as well have been a bastard.
At least that's what I always thought.
It would have been easier to explain
Than you
Only wanting people to know I belonged to you
If I
Was making you look good.

Quit honestly,
Even that wasn't enough.
MVP trophies I won
Without you in the stands.
Recitals I performed in front of hundreds
But you were not in the audience.
The game,
Some game
Was on
Somewhere.
Banquets, awards, scholarships
All things to honor
Me.
All things I worked for
To be loved by
You.

To no avail.

Then one day it came out.
Words directly from your lips.
I never wanted kids.
I don't even consider you mine.
At a restaurant in Key West.
On a family vacation
None of us wanted to be on.
But there is was
I was nothing to you.
Simply a vessel of your DNA
And nothing more.

Except,
If I was nobody,
Why did my weight matter so much to you?
Why did I have a different curfew than my brother?
Why did I have to follow your inequitable rules?
If I wasn't even yours
I should not have had a man to fear
When he was sober
But more so when he was drunk.

I should not have had to listen to

The angry

Vial

Accusations of my virtue.

The broken record that my mind adopted.

Telling me I'm weak.

I'm dirty.

I'm stupid.

I'm worthless.

Words

That for years

I have worked to unwrite from the tapestry of my mind.

Building love and worth in the body I live in.

All to silence the voice

Of a man

Who never even wanted me.

I wish

I had just been

A bastard.

I Deserved It

The laughter echoed through my bones
As I walked through the hallway
"Good, someone finally taught that stupid white bitch
a lesson!"
What lesson was that?
People will hurt you?
People will laugh at your pain?
No one cares?

The black eye and fat lip didn't generate sympathy.
Not from friends or teachers.
No one asked why my face was bruised and swollen.
Just applauded.

I was fourteen
And it was hard not to feel
Like the whole world thought
I deserved it.

A Week From Hell, Merry Christmas

Saturday

"Mom, he's not home, I can go get all of your stuff out now."

"I just feel so bad. I shouldn't be doing this at Christmas."

"There is no good time, and you have to be safe."

Sunday

"Did I hear you right? You're going away and he gets served this week?"

She brought some things over to the room I have had ready for 2 months.

Monday

I tell my staff to be prepared. If he shows up, call the police. That night I talk to him like I have for 30 years. Just enough so that he doesn't feel slighted and not so much that I get lost. Let this be the last day I have to speak to him.

Tuesday

"Can you spare an hour to get everything out?"

We pack our two cars full. You've reached adulthood when your mom moves in with you.

Wednesday

"Any news?" Nothing. "I can tell him."

My mom says, "I don't want you to put yourself in danger."

I reply, "I have places to hide." As if I hadn't been preparing for this my whole life.

My best friend is visiting. We have a game night.

My dad responds in a surprisingly calm manner.

I'm terrified.

Thursday

Christmas Eve.

Friends. Store.

I am alone.

Friday

Christmas.

Wrap the last gifts, to watch them be ripped open an hour later. Pick up the trash. Read a text message, from dad. Panic ensues. He wants to wish me a Merry Christmas, health and happiness, and he has presents for us. Can he come by?

I look to my best friend, "Do I have to respond? Do I have to see him?"

"No," he says, "It sounds like manipulation to me."

"Thank you." I needed someone to affirm that my fears were justified.

Saturday

My brother and I are going to see him. Please let this be the last time.

Planting Seeds

Part I

You always had a green thumb
Had a way with making things grow

You knew
To get fruit
You would have to plant the seeds

So you tilled the earth
Sowed the seeds
You fed
Watered
And watched them grow

But the bloom didn't look quite as you expected

See
When you tilled, it was my mind you were raking
Scrubbing me of my confidence
My belief
My joy

The seeds you sowed
Fear
Hate
Envy

You fed me
With insults
Condescending words
Many things short of nutritious

You watered me
To the point of drowning in my own loathing

And you watched me grow

Neglected

We were out on the town, as teenagers do. Past curfew, but far away from anywhere people would look to find us. My friends talked about how they had to get home or they would be in deep shit with their parents. I was the one with the car and so, taxied them home. They always said things at the close of the night, when they wanted to be out longer but couldn't, "Man you are so lucky, your parents let you do whatever you want. You could stay out all night and they wouldn't care!"

To them it sounded like heaven. What I heard was, "Your parents could not know where you are in the morning, and they **wouldn't even care**." It's not so different. Maybe not to someone whose parents, cared. But mine wouldn't even notice if I wasn't there. They wouldn't know. I mean, they didn't know that the fence was broken that separated our neighborhood from the interstate. They didn't know that when I had had too much of them, or of my brother, or of life, I would slide through the broken section, walk down to the interstate at night and just sit in the drainage tunnel as semis and cars passed overhead. Drowning out the noise in my head.

They didn't know that my best (only) friend's parents would constantly whisper about, "That poor girl." every time I would stay in her room while their family ate dinner, just so I wouldn't have to go home.

They didn't know that I couldn't afford school lunch so my friend, whose dad worked for Frito Lay, would steal the expired bags of chips and hide them in her locker. So, at lunch time I just had to sneak around the school, make an excuse if I ever got caught, and enjoy the stale chips no one else wanted. I always got sad when there were no chips waiting for me. Sometimes, I would go weeks without them. I didn't get to choose the chips even, I just depended on what would sell and what didn't.

They didn't know a lot. Because, "I'm so lucky, they didn't even care."

Planting Seeds

Part II

When I was a sprout
I just knew
You were there to care for me

As a seedling you saw a little weak thing you could
control
I was so hungry for affection
For attention
I would take your insults
And try to fix myself so you would love me

Though the growing was rough
My stem was strong and I began to bud
I grew in spite of you
Blooming towards the sun

Then you would come with garden shears
Kind words in front of strangers
Telling stories of your pride
Look at this thing you've grown
To them
You are just pruning
It's for the health of the roots

My blossoms turned to fruit
But I didn't look quite right to you

You expected a fruit
That you wanted to be shaped a certain way
A fruit
That you wanted to have a specific aroma
A fruit
That you wanted to taste sweet

But it was bitter
It was sour
And it was not yours

Raise the Bar

I wonder where your bar is set
Now that all your desires were meet
And they were not what you wanted?

I wonder if she knows
How quickly your love can change?
She will.

I try not to be bitter or sad
That you left me for better.

That you hoped, above all
That it was my fault.
I was what was wrong with us.

I know you still mean the best.
I know you still care.
It will never be enough.
It will never be the same.
I wish I never cried over you.
I wish I could say I'm okay.

I Just Wanted to be Loved

I don't know how many times
I told myself,
"If it's ever me or the kids,
I have to leave "
When your fist broke through another door,
Another wall.
When I would hear crashing sounds in the next room
Only to clean the mess of shattered glass in the
morning.
Once you were sleeping and docile.
When your words tore through me
With the intent to bring me down,
Beneath you,
In fear of you.
But you always said sorry,
That you would change,
That you loved me.

I just wanted to be loved.

Possibility

Tight around my neck
You pull me in close
Strip me of my clothes
Tell me what to do

This makeshift leash
One step past the ropes
And the blindfolds
That introduced this taboo

The blackness then
Brought peace
Security
Trust

This is lust
And rage

This blackness tells me
If I fight you
I will not see
Tomorrow

I will not breathe
Tomorrow

I will not live
Tomorrow

So, as you tighten the belt around my neck
Pull me across the room
Call me a bitch
Your bitch

I want so badly to fight you
To scream
To thrash
To run

But the blackness comes again
And I remember
The kids need their mom alive tomorrow

I let you degrade me
Belittle me
Abuse me

But I am alive
I am alive
And you don't even know
That I ever questioned that possibility

Fixer Upper

The first thing I fixed when you left
Was not me.
That is ongoing.

The first thing I fixed
Were the holes you punched in the walls.
When I patched the last hole
My tension eased.

I finally covered your tracks,
The evidence at least.
Of the life I don't want to admit I lived.

I Will Never Date an Addict Again

Have you ever looked at the person you love
And had to ask them to hold on,
For you?

Have you ever thrown out the pills,
Every time you found them?
Only to have him bring them home again?

Have you ever imagined
What you would do if you found them
No longer breathing?

Have you ever wondered
How you were going to tell your sons
That you couldn't keep their dad alive?

Or when he left,
Wondered if you really were the problem
Because he's getting better now?

Burn

I burn
I burn and get born again to build a new life

I have done this time and time again
But I have never had to teach someone how to burn

Today I burn
And from my ashes I must teach you to rise
To be born new

This magic has kept me eternal
But it's your magic now

I will find rest
In this mortal form
And I will find peace
Knowing you
Have the keys to eternity

Duran

Duran told me in 9th grade, "You won't have to live with him forever."

I never talked to my band teacher about my dad, but he knew.

My band teacher retired after my 9th grade year. So my last day of Jr. High was also his. He was a phenomenal teacher and person. I wasn't one of the kids who spent lunch in the band room or did anything more than play my instrument when I was cued to. But he noticed me. We didn't have lengthy conversations or any over the top bond like some of the other, geekier, bank geeks. And yet, on the last day of school, he tracked me down in the hallway, gave me a hug, and said, "You won't have to live with him forever. You just need to make it through the next few years." I almost cried. How did he know?

My dad came home from the last day of school and lectured me. Apparently, Mr. Duran confronted him in the teacher's lounge and told him he needs to treat me better. I was yelled at and told I shouldn't be telling people things that aren't true. I told my dad that I hadn't told Duran anything, and he came to his own conclusions about him. And even though I was yelled at. Even though, somehow everything was my fault again. I was happy. Someone noticed. Someone cared. And someone stood up for me.

Unconditional

You have shown me
What unconditional love is
Love that is there no matter how sad I get
Or how mad I get
How imperfect I am

You are there
Day in and day out
To tell me
You love me

Being Human

We are not alone.
The human experience is that of pain,
Resilience,
And rebirth.

Every person on this planet has struggles.
We all share in experience.

For most,
That is love.
Having it,
Losing it,
Being hurt by it.

For some of us it is trauma,
Survival,
A fighting spirit.

For all of us it is being human.

Growing Never Ends

The beauty of overthinking, is that you eventually figure things out. I often talk about how much I dislike feelings and prefer to reside in thought. I figured out why.

I don't like to feel, because none* of my feelings are inherently good. Whenever I access my emotional side (even when the emotions start from a good place) I always end up in the same place, "Everyone would be better off without me. I am hassle and a burden." Each time I let my emotional side take over, it ends there. And that is not a good place for me to be.

Now, in my rational brain, I know I am loved. I know that there are people who want me around, even seek out my presence. That I am not a burden. I know that I am strong and resilient. I know that I am more than the names I've been called and the rumors that have been spread. I know that I am intelligent, caring, and funny. I know that I am more than my body, and more than the things people can do with my body. I know I am brave and courageous, and I will survive. And one day, I will thrive. That is why I try to stay in my rational brain. It is the only place that I am safe from myself.

In therapy I have been taught to counter my intrusive thoughts. You have the thoughts that naturally (or conditionally) come into your head. These, natural thoughts are generally what make up your beliefs about yourself. They are the thoughts that you have had so frequently, that, whether they are true or not, they are what you believe. These are often the beliefs you go to therapy to change. (I would guess that people don't have intrusive thoughts of, "Gee, I'm great." or, "Wasn't that time spiffy?") The belief I most want to change about myself is the thing I feel when I allow feelings in, "Everyone would be better off without me. I am a hassle and burden."

I have been working hard for a few years now to change these beliefs. Those who have known me all along may have noticed that I am more emotional now. Those who didn't know how robotic I was before probably think that my current state is the epitome of cold, course, logic. I have grown so much, but I still have a lot of growing to do.

The more I let people in. The more I let my guard down. The more I ask people to hang out. That's my growth. That's me letting feelings exist. That's me living with a brain that sometimes believes, and is sometimes trying to believe, in all the things I know. It may not seem like much to most. It may seem like I am fiercely independent, but you only know that because I let you in to see the pieces of me I can't handle myself. It may seem like I want to control everything, but only because I have given enough leeway to you that you notice when I falter and try to take some back.

Now, there are still times that I will ask if I'm welcome to come along. If I'm welcome to talk to someone or share their space. There will be times when it seems like insecurity is driving me. When I'm asking for validation, affirmation, or even attention. These are the times that I am fighting those beliefs that I am trying to change. The times that I am looking for evidence to silence the feelings that come with those beliefs.

The sooner you realize that when I seem weak, I am building my strength. When you see me with stone cold strength, that is me attempting vulnerability. The sooner you will realize that this is why growth is a dance. This is why growing up, growing out, growing depth, is hard. Because no two struggles look the same, but that doesn't change what they are. We struggle, we strive, we grow, we thrive.

Why I'm Sad

Every time I see your sweet little face,
With your sweet little voice,
And you ask, "Mom, why do you sound sad?"
I break a little more.

If there is anyone who I am supposed to protect from me,
It's you and your brother.
You should not carry any of my pain.
And yet,
Each time you see me cry,
You broaden your tiny back,
Wrap your arms around me,
And tell me you love me.

You tell me I'm the best mom in the universe,
And I can't argue with you,
Because you're five
And even with all my flaws
You still think I'm the best thing that ever happened to you.

So, I try to accept it,
I really do.
I try to believe in all that you see in me,
But I'm still sad.

And I still don't have a good answer for you
When you ask why.

Under Pressure

They say diamonds are just carbon

Mixed with heat and pressure.

And if pressure can take

Little black nothing

And create the perception of perfection

In a clear, pure, crystal,

Surely, I can too.

With enough accomplishment.

My Voice Cracks

There is courage
In the crack of my voice

It is me demanding
Every so softly
My voice deserves
To be heard

It is the part of me
That can no longer
Stay silent

The resolve
To be better than yesterday

Professional Pretender

I'll pass you on the street
A smile on my face
"I'm glad you're having a good day."
Oh, the assumptions you make.

I'm bouncing around
Hype as hell
Showing energy that has no source
Other than the need to not be found out.

Hiding my true self
Hollow eyes
Behind a beaming smile
Distracting you from the reality you don't want to see.

Call it composure
Call it strength
Call it what you want
I'm a professional pretender.

Tenderness

"Put down the sword and dive right into the pain. You'll be proud of that skin full of scars…"

That's All I know So Far - Pink

This is the song that I think of when I hear the word tenderness. I have spent so much of my life fighting, defending, and arming myself, that I forgot how to be tender. She sums it up so well.

You have to put down the sword - Tear down your own walls, stop resisting everything around you.

Dive into the pain – Do the work, face your demons, and feel your shit.

You'll be proud of that skin full of scars – You have survived. It is your time to thrive. It is time to take all that you have learned and create a better world for the future. For you. For those that come after you.

Learn to be tender. For indeed, it will be your greatest strength.

Tired

I'm tired

I say

As I haven't gotten a good night's rest in weeks

That's easy to accept

I work too much

And care too much

I feel too much

You ask me how I'm doing

I say

I'm tired

You hear

I'm tired

I mean

I'm tired

Of existing

I'm tired

Of explaining

I'm tired

Of fighting

I'm tired

Of trying

I'm tired

Of wishing

Of hoping

Of begging

I'm tired

Even With You Gone

I can do this on my own
I will be happy
I will not cry today
I will grow
I will be strong
I will move on
I will be the me I thought I was when you were here
Even with you gone

On The Street

I learned
Long ago
To barter my body for safety.

I'll let you touch me this much
If it will satisfy your rage.
Then the fear you cause me
Can go back in it's cage.

Here's a piece of my heart
Tender but cold.
If I just warm it up people will like me
Or so I've been told.

Take my mind and mold it
Like a sculptor with his clay
If I do just what you tell me to
I can narrowly escape this fray.

My spine is in pieces now
Not erect and strong
You can dismantle the rest of me with your words
It shouldn't take you long

I'll give you my only leg to stand on
If you just give me your word
That you are not here to break me
I know the request sounds absurd.

But I've spent my life
Dealing pieces away
To protect me from the pain.

Take what you want
From my inventory
No two pieces are the same.

I have sold myself in this market
Since I was a child
To parents, lovers, and friends.

And each time I sell a new piece
I tell myself
This is where it ends.

I must build myself
Whole
And wait for the day
When somebody wants me
Complete

But each time
I feel
The terror set in
I end up back on the street.

Don't Buy the Bullshit

You tell me I sell myself short
And first,
I agreed with you

But I've changed my mind.

I am not who sells me short.
I am the one,
who,
My whole life
Has been told,
I am
Simultaneously
Never enough
And always too much.

The world tries to sell me lies.

I am told I am worth
Far less
Then I have determined.

I am told to cheapen myself.
To fall prey to a society
Who wants high quality
At a discount.

I am not an assembly line trinket.

I was forged in fire
And built with the course hands of a blacksmith
Made to stand the test of time.

Others are selling me short
I fight daily
Not to buy it.

Cursed

I am the woman
Cursed

To watch
Men

Settle into boyhood

Because the world
Demands nothing more of them

Courage

If I just admitted
Why I run
Why I hide
Why I'm scared
Maybe
I wouldn't have to
Run
Or hide
Or fear

But the courage it takes
For maybe
Is often times more
Than I can muster

Cold Nights

It's not that I don't
Believe
In loving yourself first

It's not that I think
That romance
Is the alpha and omega of life

I believe strongly
That each human
Should have their own drive
Own passion
Own fire
They should have boundaries
And dreams
And plans
All their own
But I will not deny
How cold the nights can be
When the days are hard
And the only person you have to depend on
Is yourself

I am Either

I am either
I am a lost cause
You shouldn't bother with me
Or
Bitch,
Watch me grow
Nothing can hold be down

I don't have an in between.

Valhalla

Just know
If my name ends up in the obituaries

I went down fighting.

And you can bet your ass
This bitch is in Valhalla!

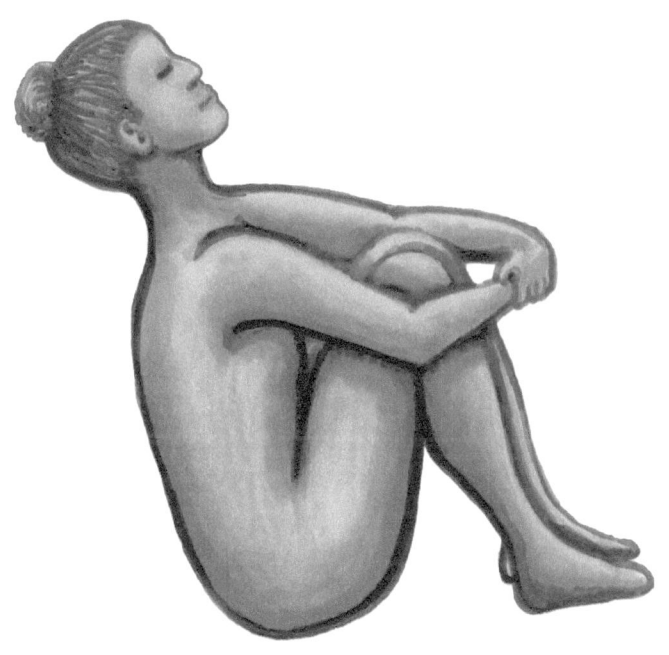

Moving

Why does this hurt so much
I have always been a vagabond
A rolling stone
I never wanted to stay put

I have always wanted
To move
To keep moving

But I don't know that it was ever a dream
But more of a nightmare
It was never about wandering and exploring
But running

Running as far away from where I came from
Never stopping
So I could never be found

It's easy to paint it as a daydream
It's easy to make yourself believe
The new paths you walk
Are out of curiosity

Until you finally feel like staying
Until that day when
What you've actually dreamt of
Comes to you

Family
Home
Community

When you finally feel like staying
But you have been found
The demons you have been running from
Are knocking at your door
And now
Now you are scared to move again

Because if you do
You lose what you have wanted
A home
A family
And a safe place to rest

Not My Voice

You'll see it in my writing,
When it's not my voice.
When words come out about me,
As if I have no choice.

I write them in italics,
To remind me,
They're not mine.
But they sound so sure of themselves
And I'm just the blind,
Leading the blind.

So what if they are right?
And I'm
Lazy and selfish
Weak and meek
A Dirty worthless whore

I can't stop them from interrupting
How do I close the door?
I know it's not me talking
And I don't want to hear it anymore.

Hey Dad

It's not that I don't think that you deserve to find someone who makes you happy and can share in love with you. It's that I don't think anyone deserves to go through what you think you have the right to put people through.

Fucked Up
Frankenstein Cyborg

I find one of my hardest challenges in life is trying to figure out how to be human. When I was young, I successfully turned off all of the living parts of me. I became quite robotic. I was highly productive, and I felt nothing.

At times I wished and hoped to feel something, because being a robot, just didn't do much for being accepted by others. I eventually (after coming to terms with what was meant for my life - solitude) learned how to be human, sort of. I still got chided for taking things too literally and for my complete lack of nuance, but I felt things. I got to take part in experiences instead of just observing them

Now I wish I could take that back. I feel like I am smooshed together pieces of facts and feelings that never show the same data. I can't calculate my way to acting like a person, and I can't feel my way to solving problems.

There are days that I am otherwise doing great and then a wave of sadness pours over me. My brain says to get up and get moving, and sometimes I can. Sometimes I can go from complete breakdown to productive employee, friend, boss, in a matter of seconds (it's a scary sight to see, I've been told). Other times, I can't be broken from the trance my emotions put me under. It is like they are constantly battling for real estate inside my head. But I have been unable to get myself back to the point of numbness. I don't know if it is my constant hope, like an addict, that I will feel happiness again. Real, true, happiness, not the muddled fake shit I feed people (and myself). Or if I broke all the mechanisms I had in place to keep things out, and they can't be rebuilt.

I am indeed the doctor and his monster, all rolled into one.

Mom, Are You Okay?

This is hard for me to say
Because I love my kids

When I got married
I wasn't ready to be a mother
Though it was a dream of mine
I thought we would be forever
But I just wanted time

He said he wanted kids
I said I wasn't ready
But he discarded my birth control on our honeymoon
and told me to hold steady

Married for just three weeks
when the test showed positive
No time to learn to be a wife
I had to learn to raise a kid

Decisions I didn't get to make
Now weigh heavy on my mind
For the women who won't get to choose
If they are ready to leave the life they know behind

I've accepted the pain that came with them as wounds
for me to heal
Knowing how they came into this world
Shatters my heart of steel

In the end keeping them was my choice
I choice I got to make
But The saddest thing I've ever heard
is their voice
When I don't know what to say

"Mom, why are you crying?
Mom, are you okay?"

Parasite Fight

You say
It's all in my head
Like that should bring me comfort

What you don't understand
Is that
My head is the most fearsome battlefield I have ever
encountered

You say
He's not the one causing my distress
It's me who is spiraling

What you don't understand
Is that
He put these thoughts here
He spent my childhood
Telling me I was weak and worthless
My adolescence
Tearing me down when I would try to stand
My adulthood
Trying to regain his control

Yes, I am strong
Yes, I have escaped from him, in reality

But the parasites he implanted in me are not real

They are immaterial

And I have dug them out from my mind and my heart

But there are remnants

There are pieces that cannot be removed

And when the phone rings, they twitch

They remember what it is like to feed on my insecurity

My self-doubt

My fear

And they hunger for more

I know I have the power to stop them

And I will

But I need you to understand

Just because I will win

Doesn't mean I don't have to fight

 # To Be A Kid Again

This feeling
This is why
When people say
Oh to be a kid again
I respond with a resounding
NO

Helpless
Worthless
Scared

That's what childhood felt like

When I was young
I couldn't escape
I couldn't leave

Now
Far away from you
And I still feel

Like a kid again

My brother reminded me

I got away from you

You aren't here

Right now

I got away

Put miles between us

But to be

All grown up

To be

Self sufficient

To be raising my own in this world

And feeling

Broken

And scared

And helpless

Even for these

Small moments

For this

Short time

Over one interaction

With you

I feel ashamed that you can still hurt me
Scare me
I should have a thicker skin than this
Isn't that why you did those things
Isn't that why

You wanted to build my character
That's what you always said

Well my character is the heroine in her dystopian
story
She has demons that resemble your face
And she will spit fire and ash before she let's you
The unlikely villain
Best her

33 Years

33 years
And he thinks
He can change my view of him
Over coffee.

Hard Truth

When I told my mom
My story
She said,
"Damn, you've got a lot of baggage."

I smiled and said,
"Yeah,
Sometimes ,
I think I would have been better off
If I were actually raised by wolves."

We laughed it off
But we both knew it was true.

Growing Conditions

It's funny how
Things will always find a way to live.

Flowers can grow through concrete.
Roots will find their way to nutrients.

Things can flourish,
No matter
How harsh their conditions are.

Owe You Nothing

Tell me I'm crazy
Tell me I'm mean
Tell me I'm stupid
Be obscene.

Tell me again dad
Why I should
Make time
To let you
Talk down to me.

You took my childhood
I owe you nothing.

Hurt That Heals

Different hurt requires different healing. But some hurt doesn't heal. I have long avoided figuring out why the pain caused by my father has led me to such unforgivability. I have forgiven a lot of unforgivable things. I have found a way to even interact with those people in a civil manner. But, with him, I can't bring myself to it.

Most of the hurt, that I have endured, though horrific in nature, has been done out of ignorance. The kids who molested me when I was little likely didn't know it was damaging to me, or even wrong. (Not to mention, it likely happened to them.) My friend from high school who raped me, 99.99% doesn't know he did. To him, it was just another romp. He was focused on his pleasure and disregarded what he had to do to get it. My ex-husband has no idea that there was a night that I was certain he was going to kill me. That I allowed him to violate me as means to get out alive. None of them were intentional about the pain they inflicted; they just didn't know any better.

My dad did so with purpose. It wasn't his lack of knowledge or experience that led him to hurt me. It was his quest for power. He would watch his words distort my brain and begin to think the thoughts he wanted me to. He would scream at me, put me down, and call me names just to watch me cower and hide from him. He would poke and pinch at me and tell me the things I need to fix, and watch me fall in line. (I am not a perfectionist by nature.)

For most of my youth I thought I was making it all up. That I was overreacting. Things couldn't possibly be this bad. These things weren't actually happening. My head was playing tricks on me. Then, when I returned from college, my cousin was living with my parents. My dad was treating her the same way. My thoughts had changed, maybe it did happen, but I was too hurt to see that it was happening to others. I talked to my older brother. I said we needed to do something. We couldn't let him treat her like he treated us. He said, "I agree, but let's be clear about this. He didn't treat us that way, he treated you that way." I felt like my pain was validated. Someone else had seen it, it wasn't in my head.

I felt less crazy, but fully enraged. It did happen. My dad spent my young life torturing me, to feel high on power. He intentionally broke me for his own amusement. I don't know that I will ever be able to see him for anything more than that.

Maybe he is trying to change. Maybe he will become a better person. But if he does, he doesn't not get to be that better person in my life. He has already taken too much from me. I will never give him the chance to play cat and mouse with me again.

Father's Day

I honestly don't know why today is so hard.
I blame social media.
All the parts about the amazing father's
And the love they give.
It just hurts.

It feels dumb that it hurts.
I know I can't change it.
I know my childhood is gone.
I know I can't get it back.
I just have to keep moving forward.

Cold

Where do you get the nerve
Selling me I'm cold?
When you are the one who threw ice
On my fiery passion.

My Family

Let me be clear
I am a kind hearted person
But I see things clearly

It doesn't matter
How many heartfelt things
You share on the internet

You can fool
Your followers
Into sympathy

You can make them believe
You have been wrongly judged
And you are the victim

But this family
You claim to
Love so much

It is my family
Not yours

And nobody fucks with my family!

Trauma Healing Is Time Travel

Take me back to who I as before.

Before I was broke,
Before I was hurt.
Before,
When I was still me.

Who is she?
I feel like we've never met.

Careful Life

"You made your choices."

I know I did
But I also know I made the choices I did
Because I was trying to escape the life I was given

I know how I got here
I know my responsibility
But I don't think I should be condemned
To a careful life
Because I had to survive throughout all the years
That most were allowed to be careless.

Sad and Alone

It's not that I'm an inherently sad person
I just get sad when I'm alone.
Because I,
Unfortunately,
Like people

The problem is that I
Am alone
A lot.
So much
That I forget how to not be.

Strength as Weakness

In conversations with friends,
in therapy,
in constant inner dialogues,
when asked what my greatest weakness is,
my answer is strength.

My strength is what keeps me distant from people,
from relationships.

My strength is what keeps me fighting people who
desire to hold me.

Strength is what has kept me safe,
but it is also what is holding me back.

I desire to be vulnerable.
I desire to be soft.
I don't know how.

I know how to battle,
to win,
to succeed,
but not to concede.

I have known from a young age
that I
am the only one who I can count on.

Unlearning that doesn't just take time.
It takes active,
exhaustive,
effort.

(*It also takes having people in your life with enough
patience and at times, endurance, to give you time to
trust in them.*)

Friend Request

Sometimes
I'm still waiting for the day
When I check up on you
To see the
"Send friend request" button
That's when I will know
You have given up on us

In This World

In this world
You are bound to have friends
Who support you
In your efforts
To drown your sorrows
In liqueur and pills

But when you try
To get better
They do not return your calls
Because the demons
You are conquering
Look a lot like they ones they can't beat

Nebula

I feel like a nebula. Like a star is trying to be born from my skin. I feel vibrations of energy bursting from me constantly. I feel I am too much for this world. I try to contain it. I want to be what I am, but I live in a human world. And to be in this world, you must be human, you can't be a star. So, I try to reign it in. I put on a face of humanity, and sometimes I almost convince myself, but this can't be contained forever. Soon my energy will expand until I engulf everything around me and burn. I will burn, and there will be no humanity that can hold me any longer.

Journey to Healing

Healing is not linear
If it were, it would resemble a heart rate
Life pulsing up and down
Flat lining and ending up lifeless.

Healing is not cyclical
It isn't a merry-go-round of constant
Reliving and learning
Until you are too dizzy to stand.

Healing is a country drive with the music turned up
Where sometimes you make four left turns, realize
you don't want to be there and drive on.
And sometimes you turn only twice because you
aren't ready to go any further just yet.
It is driving past the house you grew up in and seeing
a house and not a prison.

It is stopping for gas and snacks because you are
going to need rest and fuel to take on the long lengths
you will drive alone.
It is knowing that even if the scenery is not always
beautiful,
It is a new view with each mile marker.
Sometimes people will join you on your drive and the
conversation will be great.

Sometimes, you will turn the radio off and just listen to
the sound of tires on pavement.
But one thing I know,
The journey to healing,
Is never done.

Worth It

    I am beautiful. Not just because my looks range from naturally pretty to drop dead gorgeous but because of who I am. I am smart, funny, kind, and generous. I wear my heart on my sleeve and I love with everything I have. I try to make other people happy, because spreading joy brings me joy. I like to help people; neighbors, friends, strangers, it doesn't matter, if I can make your day better, then that is my goal. I can be one of the guys but I can also be a perfect lady. I can fix anything myself, because I've always had to, but I am learning to ask for help. I currently bench press ~~115 lbs~~ ~~155lbs~~ 180lbs, squat ~~145 lbs~~ ~~310lbs~~ 336lbs, and deadlift ~~300lbs~~ 336lbs and I love to be and to feel strong. I also love to wear dresses and sing "I Feel Pretty". I am much more than the sum of my parts. I am amazing and wonderful and awesome. And if you don't see that when you look at me, look elsewhere.

    It may have taken me a lot of heartache, a lot of time, and a divorce to make it clear. I don't want people in my life who do not add value to it. I don't want people who are just holding space in my life, that's my space. That said, if you are someone who I share my time with, it is because I see value in you and I think your existence enhances my experience on this earth. I hope I do the same for you. If I don't, feel free to have me exit stage left of your life. Whether I see something worthwhile in you, I don't want to be around you if you don't see it in me.

Witchy Woman

The more I settle into my true nature
The more I realize,
I would have been burned at the stake.

Witchy Woman

It makes sense though,
Why I feel like a phoenix.

My last life must have ended in flames.

Beautiful

I see you

When you are taking on the world

One problem at a time

And you are beautiful

Some days

The world

Seems to take more from you than it gives

And you are beautiful

I see the days when you

Have lost your patience

And you feel like you have failed

And then, you are beautiful

I get to enjoy

Watching you hoist heavy bars around

Contorting your face

Growling and grunting

And you are beautiful then too

Sometimes

You take the time for yourself

You pamper and primp yourself

Into a princess

And you are beautiful

Moral of the story

It doesn't matter

What you are doing

Or how you are dressed

You

Are

Beautiful

I Am Love

I have done the thinking

And the over thinking

The pros and cons lists

I have plotted every story

In this choose your own adventure book

And I have concluded

I am still going to be me

I am still going to give

Even if I do not receive

I am still going to care

When it feels like no one does about me

I am still going to text

To check in

To give best wishes

To cheer you on

Congratulate you when you succeed

I will still be there if you need someone

For a laugh or a cry

I will not let this world harden me
I am soft, but I am not delicate
I am kind, but I am not weak
I am love
And I will still be me

Grateful

I have learned that I can be grateful and still walk
away from you.

I want you to know
I am open to be your friend
If and when you are ready
To be what I need in a friend
But until then
I will keep my distance.
I promised I would not push.
I will not chase.
I will be grateful
For what you brought to my life.
But I will not let that trap me
Where I no longer belong.
You are welcome to meet the new me.
But you do not have a spot reserved in her life.

 *Survive*

I have been searching for answers
Trying to find the source of the strength that has
moved me through life.
Feeling so small and insignificant
Yet having power burst forth from me.

Today I was told to look inside
There, I will find my answers
Because those before me fought wars that brought
me here
And those before me live in me.

Sounds like some lion king shit, right?
It sure is
But my ancestors don't give a fuck if you think it is
silly
They have overcome more than your disbelief
And they are the source of my power
The cause of my pride
The reason I will always survive.

Shield Maiden

I've been letting go
Of things
That aren't mine

That aren't
Meant for me

With the hopes
That the next door will open

And this would be
A fine way to live
If I
We're a fair maiden
Waiting for her prince

But I do not carry this sword
To be saved
I do not carry this shield
To seek the protection of others

So, I will let go
Of what is not mine

And I will charge through this world
Of wreckage
And terror
Bloodied but unbowed

Until I get
What is

I Am Poetry

When struck with pain
A cut upon my skin
Words flow from my wound.

When sadness consumes me
It may look to you like tears
But it is words that flow from my eyes.

When lust overcomes me
And pleasure is all I seek
It is words that drip between my thighs.

I AM poetry.

Permission

Sometimes
I look in the mirror
And see just how beautiful
I am

And I think it's a shame
To think
No one will ever be able
To call my beauty their own

That I will not
Belong to another

It is a shame
That such beauty
Will go on
Wasted

Then I remember
I am much more
Than beautiful

And I remember
That I
Can admire myself
Without anyone's permission

Heavy

I used to be weighed down
By carrying the weight
Of how other people
Touched my life.

I have since
Removed their grasp.
Only fingerprints remain.

But now,
I carry a new weight.
That of the responsibility
Of taking care of myself
Like no one ever has.
Like no one else could.

I Deserve

I deserve to feel safe
To be able to be all of me
To find a place I can lay down my sword and rest.

I deserve honesty
To know that I can trust your words and actions
Enough that they ground me when I can't trust myself.

I deserve to be loved
Even when I don't feel like I'm enough
And when I feel I'm too much
When I'm at my weakest and need support
When I'm at my strongest and need nothing
And everywhere in between

I deserve to have the life I have been missing.

Fly

Sometimes,
You must fall
To fly.

So, fall.

Fall,
Utill your wings
Catch wind
And ride that currant
Until your wings
Give out.

Canvas

First take pen to paper
Then take ink to skin

Pour your soul out word by word
And let it all sink in

The words first born from you
Now rest upon your flesh

You started as the artist
And finished,
The canvas.

Eye of the Beholder

A friend once said to me, "You always refer to yourself as a dark person, but you seem to see such beauty and brightness in things. How can that be?"

I believe people should carry their own load. Because of this, my darkness, as I refer to it, isn't something that I carry in the open. It is not something for the world to deal with, but for me. When I was young, I carried it in the open, like a shield. I used it to protect me from further harm. I let my darkness make me coarse, cynical, and mean. It was a tool to safeguard myself. No one could hurt me if I didn't let them close enough. Spoiler alert, people can still hurt you from a distance.

As I have grown, I have realized that it takes more courage to be soft, more strength to be open, and more resilience to be kind. My darkness isn't for the world. My daemons are mine and mine alone. I am the one who must face them, to defeat them, or learn to live with them.

No one can fight for you, they can, however, assist you in your fight. Whether it's a therapist helping you to safely uncover your daemons and teaching you how to cope with them. Or a friend to notice when you are lost in your head and pulling you back to safety. Having people in your corner can make or break your ability to fight your darkness. They can't touch your darkness, but they can provide the strength you need to do so.

Samwise couldn't carry the ring for Frodo, but he could carry Frodo.

The people you choose to be in your life have a huge impact on who you become. "You are the average of the 5 people you spend the most time with." - Jim Rohn . Though the limit is not at 5, you do become what you surround yourself with. Choose wisely, spend your time with purpose. Everyone needs a friend who will wield a battle axe for them, but you should also know who you will pick up the axe for.

Everything has beauty. Too many people overlook it. A metallic beetle, a springy root, a real conversation; They all enhance our earthly experience. We get lost in what beauty is supposed to look like. Whether it is clothes, hair, selfies, shiny new tech. There are plenty of things that can draw your eye, but looking isn't seeing, just as hearing isn't listening. Anyone can scratch the surface, few dive into the depths.

I have been given the power to appreciate things that few appreciate. I **see** things that most only **look** at. Someone has to recognize that weeds are just resilient flowers that don't know how to, not survive. Someone has to see that people make mistakes, but that doesn't make them inherently bad. Someone has to realize that light means nothing without the dark, and you need both to see clearly.

Life – A Maze

As I walk this labyrinth
Desperate to escape,
The twists and turns confound me
My life I must reshape.

Build brick by brick
A life I can love
Learn and grow
Into something I'm proud of.

Years of work
I look on appraising
Finally, I feel it's true.
Life's a-maze(ing).

Merely a Vessel

The words I write may come from my pen
I may be the one with ink-stained fingers
But I am merely a vessel

These words already exist
These thoughts are already formed
I just let them flow from me

When a flowing poem forms a stream
A growing poem forms a tree
It is not me

I am not a wizard
Transforming words into wonder
I am a vessel
A catalyst
A ferryman

I am the bridge from thought to existence
Merely a vessel
And nothing more

Hollow

For the first time

In a long time

I didn't feel alone

I felt like a had someone in my corner

And now that corner is empty

Maybe there was too much pressure

To fill my emptiness

Even though I told you

It wasn't your responsibility

Now that emptiness feels

Hollow

Dark

Daunting

Safety and Fear

Sometimes I still imagine spending time with you.
Not because I want you
But because your face still reminds me of safety.
And sometimes I still want to feel safe.

The truth is
You made me feel safe.
Safety is not a commodity I'm used to
But I got used to it
Because of you.
Then you were gone
And I've had to learn
How to live with fear again.

Careful What you Wish For

Some say you only get from the universe what you ask for.

I asked for a life full of people who value me.
I received an exodus of people who said they cared but showed they didn't.

I really hoped they would be the ones
But now I know they weren't.
And they had to clear that space
To make room for what is to come.

To get what you want,
You have to lose what no longer serves you.

He Killed Me

I think about our conversation
Every time I hear someone
Comment on someone who stayed
Every time I hear someone say,
"They should just leave him,"
Or, "It's a shame she'll never leave him,"
Or, "She keeps going back to him."

When I hear people comment about things
They don't understand!
But I understand.
And I remember when I told you
That him leaving me
Was the best thing that ever happened to me.
Because I knew,
In my heart,
That if he hadn't left me,
I would have stayed until he killed me.

Tattoo Tapestry

I once heard someone say
"Don't date a girl with tattoos,
It's a sure sign of trauma."

I don't disagree
I don't know anyone who would pay for needles to
puncture them 1,000 times
Who hasn't survived more

But every tattoo has a story
A meaning
Even the most ridiculous

My story,
Is that of strength.
Each design left within my skin
Is a symbol of what keeps me going

Family,
Friendship,
And refusing to let my story end on anyone else's
terms

Whoever said that a tattooed girl was damaged
Wasn't wrong
They just forgot to mention
That our tattoos are the treasure map
To show you how we survived
And how we've healed.

Backsliding

Sometimes you must back pedal.

Sometimes you must slip.

Sometimes you must fail.

Sometimes you must remember what it looks like

falling to the bottom again.

To remember why you have been climbing,

Tooth and nail,

To get out of the pit.

Look up.

Keep looking up.

That is where you will see the light.

The sun is shining.

Don't stop reaching until you get there.

A beautiful life awaits you.

Atlas

I know how heavy life is
I am not in the habit of acting like it's not
I am in the habit of lifting it over and over
Until I'm strong enough
To hold it all on my shoulders
With the composure of Atlas

Firefighter

I had a therapist once tell me that I was a firefighter because no matter what was happening, I would always jump right back into the flames. It happened in relationships, friendships. I was what I called peoples' 'crisis friend'.

Anytime the world was falling apart I was the person that they called because I'm a great problem solver. Or as I've come to learn, I have been living through trauma my entire life and so I roll with the punches really well. (Except for that one time in 8th grade, I got a couple bruises from that one.)

However, the biggest thing I've ever done in my firefighter role was when my little brother was born. I moved back to the hometown that I spent 10 years working to get out of and planned on never coming back to. Because I needed to protect him from my dad.

It took 12 years before I convinced my mother to leave my dad. 12 years of my younger brother's life, 33 years of mine. It has been a rough fucking year and it's not done yet.

But one thing that makes me happy is when I moved my mom and little brother into my house, my mom asked him how he liked the living situation and he said, "It's fun and I feel safe," and if there is one thing that I could offer to people, especially people who I care about deeply, is safety.

Because for fuck sake, if I can be somebody's safe place, so be it! If it means that I must be hurt and be pummeled and jump into fires that aren't even my fires so that other people can feel safe, fuck yes!

But I'm also learning how to keep myself safe in the process and that has been a very difficult lesson to learn.

Patch the Holes

It took me nearly four years to patch every hole in the wall that he put there. Replace the doors that were broken. I started with the ones I had to see every day, and covered the others up. I patched them, but didn't finish them properly. So, like scars, in the right light you can still see them. It was the first thing I did when he moved out. I thought about the shards of glass I swept up over the years. The belongings that don't belong to anyone now, because they were broken and thrown out.

For years, I had friends tell me that my relationship was abusive. They said I shouldn't be ashamed; their first husband was too. That's how they knew. They knew because I would tell them the mean, hateful things he said, the put downs and the threats. And I would tell him how sweet he became afterward. He was really sorry and would make it up to me. They told me that was how the cycle worked. I didn't believe them.

I didn't believe that I was in an abusive marriage. Just as I didn't believe I was raped. It took weeks of my therapist asking me if I consented to sex with Michael, if I said no or stop. It took me reading the pages and pages of poems and prose I wrote when I got home that night. Reading my own words about how I didn't want to, how I said no and stop. But I still didn't believe it. Until I did. I didn't believe that my husband abused me, until he left, and I knew what life was like without abuse again.

I remember being the girl who said, he's never hit me while reminding myself that if it was ever me or the kids I had to leave. I remember what it felt like to have some freedom, then fighting for the rest when he changed his mind and wanted to come back. I said no.

For years, I thought I was mean for considering him abusive, even after the night I thought he was going to kill me. I thought I should have stuck it out longer and helped him heal. It was unfair of me. But as I was watching Maid on Netflix a character said, "Before they bite, they bark." And I knew I did the right thing. I knew that if he hadn't left me, I would still be in an abusive marriage. I would have been too broken down to get out. My world would look so different.

You leaving,
Was the best thing
That ever happened to me.

Work It Out

I remember the day you said we could work things out. I sat at the edge of your bed that now took up our office. You said if I still loved you we should try. You wrapped your arms around me and enclosed me in a hug. My skin turned to needles, my stomach to knots, and tears flooded down my face.

"No! I don't trust you!"

To be embraced by someone you love but don't trust may be the most painful feeling I've ever felt. My body turning to stone under the pressure of my own thoughts.

Exhausted

I'm exhausted
Being the parent if two little boys
Who I desperately want
To grow into good men
Who are able to feel
While still being resilient enough to survive this world.

Acting as a co-parent to my little brother
Who has a decade of bullshit to undo

Reassuring and parenting my mother
Who in 55 years
Has never been on her own
Who doesn't know
That she can be
Whatever she wants

And lastly,
Reparenting myself
To teach myself
That I deserved
Much more than I ever thought I was allowed.

I always wanted a family
But parenting 5 on my own
Is exhausting.

I Wanted More

I wanted
More from my life
Than healing
The wounds
The world has
Placed upon us
So that
The future
Doesn't have to feel them

Uprooting

I have always dreamed
Of having roots
And taking flight

Exploring the great beyond
And returning home

But I have long lacked
A home to return to

I spent so long running form my past
I never thought I would find a home.
Until I built one for myself.

I have been planting roots.
And preparing to fly.

Then my past showed up at my door.
Ready to rip me from the ground.

I must remember,
These are my roots,
I planted them,
I shall tend to them.

Theses are my wings,
I can spread them
Or tuck them away.

But I do so
At my command.
Not out of fear
Of what can't hurt me anymore.

Teeth

Never tell me that children need to learn
To take care of themselves
That life is unfair
And the sooner they learn
The better

The world has teeth
And I will not
Let it
Sink those teeth
Into my kids

Because it has
Already
Taken its pound of flesh from me

Wish Me Luck

The world isn't as hard as we made it ,
I wish someone would have taught us that.

I'm trying to teach my kids.
Trying to find a balance between preparing them to
survive in the world that is,
While preparing them to make it a better place.

Wish me luck.

My Way Home

Much like I can still find my childhood home by
memory
So too
Can I find you
For you have lain in this spot since I was fifteen
Nineteen years
Millions of tears later
I will visit you
Until I no longer remember
My way home

The Point

I never meant to hurt you.
But I guess that's kind of the point.
Humans make mistakes
And sometimes
Those mistakes hurt others.

Safety

Safety is gravely overlooked. Especially, the feeling of safety derived from others. Safety you don't have to fight for. Because safety you must fight for is just fear and living in fear may keep you safe, but it doesn't feel like safety.

We are social creatures, whether we like it or not. We are pack animals. We are not made to weather the storms alone, but many of us do. Many of us don't know any other way to remain safe, because it's those who were supposed to protect us that hurt us. So, when comfort and safety are given, we reject it out of fear.

That brings up distrust. We may have people in our lives that would be there for us if we ask. We may have people who stand up for us when we are not around. We may have people who make our lives safer. That does not always mean we feel safe. Some people bring the feeling of safety and security with them and that feeling matters. Feeling safe gives us the opportunity to relax and let down our guard. Unfortunately, the people who feel safe don't always have your safety in mind, and they hurt you. Unintentionally. Then we learn that fear keeps us safe better than comfort. But we still long for comfort.

Red Flags

I don't know if I'm making up red flags because I am
scared

or if I am ignoring red flags because I am happy

No Longer My Problem

I chose to stop drinking alcohol because I could sense myself turning to self-destructive habits again and adopting the most socially accepted addiction of all was sure to go unnoticed. I did not announce my sobriety to the world. I simply told my friends as it came up, "No thank you, I don't drink anymore." And instead of hearing support or encouragement from my friends I have heard, "Yeah, but you can still drink with me, I'll take care of you." "Are you sure you won't just drink one White Claw, it's not the hard stuff." "I would feel a lot more comfortable if you had at least a little bit of liquor in you."

It seems that my friends don't understand that in order for me to do what is in the best interest of my health, both mental and physical, I have to make decisions for me. I can no longer live my life based on what makes other people feel more comfortable. If you feeling guilty for drinking when I am not, that is your demon to face, not mine. I will no longer hurt myself for your comfort!

Sobriety

I think

Maybe

I chose sobriety

Because then

If I start spending all my time

Drinking and partying

Maybe someone will notice

That I'm not being myself

Maybe then

Someone will notice

I am calling out for help

Planting Seeds

Part III

How did you not know
Fear cannot bear sweet fruit
Hate does not create a pleasant aroma
Envy will not craft the perfect shape

The seeds you planted had no chance to grow for you

And yet

I ripen

My fruit
Is sweet

My aroma
Succulent

My shape
Tender
Yet firm

The seeds you planted could not grow for you
But they have flourished for me

Proud

I see kids I went to school with as adults, and I want
to give them a hug and tell them I'm proud of them.
They are never people I was particularly friends with.
Just the ones that wore the same expressionless
faces as me.
I always wondered, what is it for you?
Do your parents do drugs?
An alcoholic father too?
Did you grow up too fast at the hands of someone
else?
Are you raising your younger siblings or working to
pay the bills?
I always wondered what battle they were fighting.
What war raged on in their head.

Then I see them at a little league game with their kids.
Smiles on all their faces.
And I want to give them a hug and tell them I'm proud
of them.
Because it is not easy to come from that life and end
up with a smile on your face.

Story

If how we are remembered
And what makes us eternal
Is our story

I'm going to go ahead
And write my own.

Sleep

I sleep
More often than not
These days.

There are still
Nightmares
And night terrors
Once in a while.
They make for rough days.
But mostly,
I sleep.

A Whole New World

I refuse to let you live in the world I grew up in.
So, I have chosen to build a new one.
One where you can grow
In whatever direction you desire.
Where you come home to safety
Instead of more fear.

I do not need to be a barrier to overcome
You will have plenty of those.
I will instead be the voice in your head
That reminds you,
You will get through this.
You are resilient.
And the world is yours for the taking.

Well Worth It

I love that my children
Can tell me stories
Of their escapades
With no idea of the things
That weigh heavy on my heart

I may be a lost cause
But if it means they
Get to have a joyous life

It is well worth it.

 *Pillows*

I have always slept with one pillow
And one blanket
With the temperature turned down.

I have always been a minimalist.

Not in my design aesthetic
Or Zen like way of existing
But in the sense that I only ever allowed myself what I
needed to survive.

I've always been frugal.

Not in my budgeting ability
Or investment prowess
But that I didn't consider food a necessity.

I have always been an early riser.

Not to seize the day
Or get a jump on the competition
But because 3am is the alarm set by my anxiety.

I have always known
Comfort kills.
The early bird gets the worm.
Nobody cares, work harder.

I have always known
A penny saved is a penny earned.
And having anything more than nothing
Gives you something to lose.

I remember it like it was just yesterday

When working harder was more important than sleep.
When saving money was more important than eating.
When surviving was more important than being
healthy.

I bought 3 new pillows for my bed yesterday
And I slept past sunrise.

Shining My Light

I wonder
If anyone realized
That I shine brightest
When I'm engulfed in darkness

If,
Instead of basking in my light
They turned to help me
They would have seen my struggle

Instead
They reaped the benefits
Using my despair
To lessen their own

Treat Me Well

I want routine
Without obsession
Is that too much to ask?

Not to fear
Myself
For making changes

To trust
That I can
Treat myself better

That I love myself enough
Now,
To treat me well.

Knew Me Happy

I really wish you knew me happy.

Secure in myself and happy.

It's a game changer.

I Grew

I'm not going to apologize
For becoming
The person
You told me
I was capable of being.

I'm not going
To hold back
Because I outgrew you

I am not going
To make people comfortable
Anymore
By contorting myself
To fit their acceptable image

Choke

I have spent my life
Cutting myself into
Bite size pieces
So as to make sure
I was never too much
For anyone

No more

I am all of me
If you can't handle it
You can choke motherfucker!

Wild Horse

It's hard to picture,
I'm sure.

People see me in my strength,
In my fortitude,
And they assume I have always been this way.

When I tell them,
I couldn't leave if I tried.
That I accepted the assault
And the fear.

They don't believe,
I was broken.
A wild horse who was too afraid to leave the stable.

You don't see it now,
Not because I hide it,
I have given up on being ashamed,
But because I have stitched my wounds together.
Scar tissue has formed under the surface.
Gnarled and painful but holding me together.

When the stable burned down,

I finally realized,

The horizon was my home,

And the walls around me were merely ash.

Forest Fires

Only you can prevent forest fires!
As my mind embers around ideas of fear, sadness,
and pain.
I do not try to stoke them
Yet somehow, they grow with force.
The slightest breeze
Be it comment or action
Will grow the ember to a flame.
Finding every piece of kindling
Dead dreams, memories and dried tears.
Each catching flame to grow the danger.
As the fire grows,
It is not just the barren things that burn.
The age-old evergreens that tower over the forest, the
saplings, the ground cover,
Each the secure parts of me being charred black.
Scarred by the parts of me I have not healed.

My friends jump in
Ready to fight back the flames.
Pouring water from the sky,
Building fire lines of resilience
With bulldozers of affection, adoration, and
affirmations.

And yet,

As I try to breathe,

I instead choke on smoke and soot.

False beliefs that are so ingrained in me

I do not know them to be untrue.

The firefighters keep at the flames

For days,

or weeks,

or more.

Rain, pouring like tears from the gods,

Helps,

Until the fire finally dies out.

Which it always does.

The smoke dissipates from the air.

The ash settles to the ground.

The sky returns to blue,

Not a crimson haze.

The land lies barren.

Charred and scarred by the wrath it carried.

Often, it will look this way for years,

Decades even.

Until one day

Saplings grow.

Healing happenings.

And with time,

A forest stands again.

I am Whole

I am the kind of woman
Who needs someone who is whole.
On their own.

I am not in the business
Of piecing together puzzle pieces
To see if they fit.

I am whole
On my own.
And when I have entertained people
Who were trying to find their missing pieces.
They took away from me,
To try to fix themselves.

I do not want to be less than.
I do not wish to take away
Any of what makes me
Me.
Because I love me.

I need someone who is whole.
So, that I can be my whole self,
And love their whole self.
Without compromise.

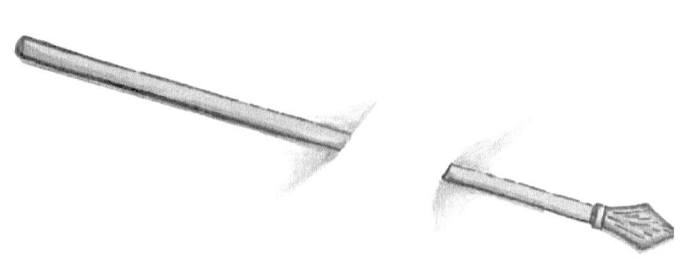

Victim vs Survivor

In this day and age, you hear a lot of talk about victim mentality and how people should become survivors instead. I would argue that you need to be both. People would like to say that anyone who reacts as a victim has a victim mentality, I think there is a distinction.

You see, someone with a victim mentality will always feel like things were someone else's fault. Victims usually feel like things were their own fault. They should have been smarter or stronger. They should have done something to prevent what happened to them. Those with a victim mentality can make poor decisions and blame the world for their consequences.

The fact of the matter, though, is that when people are hurt by others, they are victims. If you are assaulted by another person, you are a victim of assault. If you are beaten by someone you are a victim of violence. If you are talked down to and belittled by someone you are a victim of emotional abuse. Calling it what is it can help you overcome it.

You cannot be a survivor without first being a victim. How quickly you move form victim to survivor is variable. For most it is a dance. Some days you are in the same, weakened state, that you have when you were hurt by someone else. Some days you are a brave soul fighting back anything that has ever tried to hurt you. One day you are victim, the other a survivor. You do not have to be one or the other. You must be both. To be a survivor, you must be able to admit that you were a victim and you prevailed.

I Fired My General Today

There was a mob of screaming faces, all resembling my own, looking towards me to make a move. To direct them to safety. Some of them were angry, others scared. Some just didn't know they could be anything but enraged. I realized that they expected a war. They were ready for war. They always had been.

It could be because the person who always stood next to me, guiding me, was the general of my army. A fearsome warrior who had never taken a loss. Not one she couldn't come back from at least. I knew, to calm the mob, I had to remove her from her post.

I turned my back to the crown, walked up to the General and said, "Thank you for everything you have done for us. You have protected us through every battle. Won every war. You have been the backbone of this kingdom. I am indebted to you. However, we are not at war anymore. We have to learn how to live without seeing the world as our enemy. It's time to rest."

She simply crossed her arms and looked at me like a disdainful child, "You're going to regret this," she growled, and walked away.

I turned toward the crowd and told them that we were going to stay here for a while. Get to know each other. And find peace. They looked puzzled, but I trusted that they would find their way. Once the courtyard calmed, I walked down the steps into a long hallway that led to a dressing room. I knocked. A raspy voice answered.

I walked in to see a large silhouette of samurai battle armor, the general's garb. Her back was to me as we spoke. "I know who you are," I said. "You are not a battle-hardened warrior or a heartless mercenary. You are just a child. You should not have to be at the front lines of every fight."

She turned to face me, looking like a comic version of everything I'd ever seen of her. Her garments were undone in the front to reveal a robot-like contraption made to impose her stature on the world. She stood on stilted legs strapped to her feet, and had pillows stuffed between her and the armor she carried. Her helmet rested squarely on the shoulders of her armor. "I am the only one who protected us through all those battles. Without me, we wouldn't have survived!"

She was right, so I told her, "I know. That doesn't change the fact that you never should have had to do that."

She began to take off her suit of armor. "So, what now, am I just supposed to lay down and let the world destroy me after I fought so hard to be here?"

"No, absolutely not. But when was the last time you had to fight?" She had no response. "When was the last time you used your sword?" Still no answer. "Doesn't that armor get heavy wearing it day in and day out?" As she stepped out of her costume, she had the look of an aged warrior, but on a child's face. "The armor will always be here, but that doesn't mean you have to bear the burden of it all the time."

She looked up at me, her feet on the ground, barely four feet tall and said, "What would you have me do?"

"Well, to start, will you go for a walk with me?" She looked down at what she was wearing, a chest plate that seemed to have become one with her. "Don't worry, you can keep that on." I reached out my hand and she reluctantly took hold.

As we walked outside, there was a glowing golden light that surrounded us. First, we walked through a meadow filled with wildflowers, chirping birds, and buzzing bees. I could feel her arm relax. We passed by a willow tree looking over a pond. As we looked over the edge, she saw her reflection. The face of a perfect, innocent child looked back at her. At first, she seemed shocked. It was unlikely that she had looked at her reflection much over the years. But then she was in awe. She saw a face that she had forgotten about, and she could not stop staring. A frog jumped out at her and she jumped and giggled. She looked at me, "Should we keep going?"

As we walked, we talked. I showed her pieces of my life. People who I trust, who make me feel safe. I showed her times that we got hurt, but we healed. I showed her that we are strong and capable and unafraid of the battles we may have to fight. I showed her some of the dark times. The times she helped us get through. But then I showed her the pain that carrying those battles caused us. And I showed her how relieved we were when we set down our sword. Even if it was only for a moment.

Along our walk we came upon a playground. Lying on the ground was a jump rope. She let go of my hand and picked it up. With both handles in her hands, she swung the rope over her head and jumped, but she could not get over the rope. She tried a few more times before she turned to me, "It is really hard to jump with this heavy armor on. Can you hold it for me?"

"I would love to. I will keep it safe for you. Play." As I held her chest plate, I watched her, jump rope, and run to swings and slides. Screaming, giggling, tripping over her own feet, and promptly returning to play. I smiled with tears in my eyes. She was the epitome of joy.

She ran up to me breathless, "This is so fun! But where are the other kids? I want someone to play with."

My happy tears turned sad. "There are no other kids here. They've all grown up."

Her face sank. "Then can we stay here? Just you and me? We can play together!"

I felt like a mother who had broken a promise, "We can't stay here forever, I still have work to do. But I will find you some kids to play with. I will. I will find people who you can be safe to be a kid with. I will find time for you to be a kid. Deal?"

She looked suspicious, "You promise?"

"I promise."

She looked back at the playground, took a deep breath and reached for my hand as she led me back to the path that took us there. We just walked as I carried her armor under one arm and held her hand with the other.

Meet the Author

C. S. Phoenix is a certified life coach, athletic coach, and proud single mother of two. A BIPOC and LGBTQI+ ally, Phoenix is a strong advocate of open communication, empathy, and regaining power through vulnerability. When she isn't working or writing, Phoenix enjoys gardening, driving through the mountains, and playing a variety of sports. In the future, she hopes to travel to every continent and continue to bring courage to others by opening up about her own experiences.

csphoenix.com

@c.s.phoenix

Illustrator

Rachel Ross

Rachel is a multimedia artist with works in clay, acrylic paint, watercolor, ink, and other water-based mediums. She is an avid dog lover and water-skiing enthusiast. When she is not working, she is creating art, camping, or reading fantasy novels.

rachelmross.com

@rachelross87

www.ingramcontent.com/pod-product-compliance
Lightning Source LLC
Chambersburg PA
CBHW020253130626
46549CB00005B/2197